Summer's Child

poems by

Sharon Scholl

Finishing Line Press
Georgetown, Kentucky

Summer's Child

Copyright © 2016 by Sharon Scholl
ISBN 978-1-944899-37-0 First Edition
All rights reserved under International and Pan-American Copyright Conventions. No part of this book may be reproduced in any manner whatsoever without written permission from the publisher, except in the case of brief quotations embodied in critical articles and reviews.

ACKNOWLEDGMENTS

By Chance is published in *Rats Ass Review*, Fall, 2015.
Love at 80 was published in *Third Wednesday*, summer, 2014.
Uncle Harold and Anatomy Lesson were published in the Family collection of the *LA Writers Tribe*, 2015.
Reading Reminisce Magazine was published by *Mason's Road* in their Memory issue, 2015.

Editor: Christen Kincaid

Cover Art: Public Domain collection at depositphotos.com; Screen 2 Dandelions

Author Photo: Sharon Scholl

Cover Design: Elizabeth Maines

Printed in the USA on acid-free paper.
Order online: www.finishinglinepress.com
also available on amazon.com

Author inquiries and mail orders:
Finishing Line Press
P. O. Box 1626
Georgetown, Kentucky 40324
U. S. A.

Table of Contents

Hometown 1

Fully-Loaded 2

Summer's Child 3

Uncle Harold 4

From the Back Porch 5

Calling Long Distance 6

Driving the Teen-Ager 7

Ocala Forest 8

Neither Snow Nor Rain 9

By Chance 10

Dirge 11

Inheritance 12

Acts of Mercy 13

Love at Eighty 14

Ghostwalk 15

Reading Reminisce Magazine 16

In Retrospect 17

Small Deaths 18

Azalea Ladies Club 19

Anatomy Lesson. 20

Hometown

This morning I'm back
where my whole young life

dribbled out with books and bikes,
school bags and dancing shoes.

The route to the bus stop
engrained in my bones, each house

a dimpled groove upon my brain.
I find my town plowed down,

built up, mowed, planted,
bricked up, cemented in, rerouted,

detoured, bridged, tunneled,
excavated, filled in, leveled,

stacked, fenced and pedestrianized.
I kept saying I'd come back one day—

but when I did, it wasn't there.

Fully Loaded

I've memorized this road by twist
and vista. I could drive
it blind by warmth
of light across my shoulders,
successive smells of goldenrod,
hay and creek mint.

At this bend, in the metal bed
of daddy's pickup, wobbling
side to side, we cousins tumbled
like loose timber
rattling with laughter.

Below the hillcrest, the broken
rectangle of rock marks my first
house, warped limbs of my apple
tree hugging chimney ruins.

My father's hearse bumped down
that lane to the country cemetery
unmarked on maps.

My car goes slower every year,
engine groaning from the load
of all these people,
all that time.

Summer's Child

Two velvet pillows,
my small tanned legs straddled
starch-white thighs
of grown-up laps.

Their skin revealed like tracing
paper every shattered
vein, each dimpled
glob of fat, their figured dermascape
of moles and wrinkles.

Smooth as chocolate
milk, mine were sun-browned
from endless days
spent roaming creek sides,
scaling trees.

Theirs stayed white
from hose and trousers,
curtained windows,
dark spaces under desks.

I never knew how much they paid
for my idle days that edged
gently into twilight,
summer rising over me
like a green umbrella.

Uncle Harold

As I flew up, your arms inscribed
the great arc of the universe,
my child-head wreathed with clouds
and dreams, laughter spilling
from the crucible of my joy.

Your presence blew
into our house, censing us with cigar
smoke, your voice like gravel bouncing
off the walls.

I see you now draped in sterile sheets,
your skin like yellow porcelain,
arms thin as water pipes, voice rattling
with phlegm.

You look at me with milky eyes
through cataracts, deaf to my voice
calling you back.

I want to be there again
locked in your godlike grip,
circling up and up
where earth falls
away and time forever ceases.

From the Back Porch

Too early up, too bleary
to read my watch.
Light here breaks
before I'm queued to it,
pale gray by five a.m.
We're closer
to everlasting summer days
that fade
but hardly blacken.
Plants work to exhaustion,
spreading their Persian carpets
even over sand
at Saint Simon's Inlet.
The relentless noise
of manufacture: cells dashing
through leaf veins,
leaves breaking from branches,
caterpillars chewing vegetation,
the aural footfalls
of a million insects
traversing a tree.
The moan and pop
of trees like old men
bending in the wind—
all this is mystery,
the wandering of a mind
pulled from sleep.
Listening at that level,
how could I survive the din?

Calling Long Distance

My whole head
is shot through with your voice

pouring from a vague
dimension that contains,

defines you.
Your speech sounds

weary, having leapt
great mountains

and squeezed into the shape
of your projected

presence. You are
stuck at a place

between thought
and fact, so diaphanous

I cannot think its name.
Our laughter dances

on that ledge of possibility.
In the after-silence

I hear this indefinable
swallow you like arctic

darkness and bear
you off to mystery.

Driving the Teen-Ager

She would prefer something
with a button,
lever, keypad, a robot
that doesn't speak.

To her, I am a junkyard of mis-
information, dead dreams,
insignificant topics
that cannot be salvaged.

She has forgotten the bulk of school
vocabulary, pared her begrudged
 responses down to monosyllables.

Some distant world
clothes her in a space suit
zipped against the foreign, repellant
atmosphere of mine.

Unnoticed as window pane,
I am ghost hands
upon a steering wheel,
a slab of raw utility.

Ocala Forest

Something in me   beyond seeing
seeps into knowing
        finding fragments
stitched together by leaves   threads of moss
green banners shaking against sky
spelling something   indistinct
in archaic runes

Forces in me trembling
like an eager animal   smelling prey
earth odors mummy-wrapped
        around my spirit
a drum of sound rhythmed to my heart
bird calls   mammal cries
        a web of counterpoint

I am here   a presence palpable
sensors on alert
        Nothing needs to happen
it is enough to be   to have eyes drunk on seeing
ears vibrating
        possessed by this space
this world flowing through me

Neither Snow Nor Rain

Yawning in too early
light, an old

gossip full of news, tongue dripping
election ads
commercial come-ons.

Tipsy on one leg, it leans
streetwise
wobbly in strong wind.

Mottled gray, gone back to woodland
squirrel perch

it resists
the rush to instant messaging

the morass of tweets and twitters. Here
with the horses

it intends to stay. I'm still
thrilled to see a familiar
scrawl tumble from its

mouth on an envelope
that smells like someone's kitchen.

By Chance

My grandson bursts through the door,
his smile vibrating like a jar of shaken candy.

No reason he is here, safe,
splitting his seams with another year's growth,

not gray-stiff in a sinking grave
with me bent like boneless flesh upon the dirt.

No reason I am here, braced
against the flying leap of his small

ecstatic body. I could be trembling
with frailty, pillows at my crumbling back.

We are accidents of time, whenever
now is, my small fraction of forever,

coincidence of place, wherever
home turned out to be.

I revel in the solid smack
of his chest slamming me windless.

Dirge

Grandma loved the Versailles elegance
of coffins displayed in draped parlors.

She craved the Byzantine formality
of receiving lines, the burnished

elegance of gilt-edged prayer books.
Grandma learned funereal whispers, tones

tremulous at phrase ends,
the precise pressure of clasped

hands dispensing sympathy.
She longed to be wept out to courtly

gestures of lace handkerchiefs
and revived with reception edibles.

Grandma was a priestess in grief's liturgy,
practiced in the intricacies

of its cantilena. She died in Bible
and long gloves, reading the obituaries.

Inheritance

Aunt Mary shimmers through the fragile
surface of her cut-glass platter.
It is the only fragment
I can grasp to hold her
to this world.

Aunt Margaret's taco recipe wafts
me back on chili vapors, her spacious
kitchen with a haze of family voices
stuck forever to the walls.

I still wear Mama's camisoles
my back curved to fit
just as hers did. Straps
slide like migrant tendrils
down my shoulders.

My house is full of ghosts
sleeping in old bowls,
singing in the hourly clang
of an ancient clock.

I'll live a half-life on shelves and porches
of my children's houses, but I doubt
I'll mind being remembered
as a chair.

Acts of Mercy

He pulls her socks on carefully
over toes angled as tree limbs,
pulsing with a steady ache.

He threads her sweater onto arms
V-shaped and trembling
with the unquelled rhythm of disease.

Feet braced against her weight,
he heaves her upward where she clings,
wet paper hanging from the wall rail.

They stumble down the hall,
his foot nudging hers into place,
his arm urging her body to lurch forward.

A ceaseless ritual like Muslim prayer,
night and morning intractable,
funneling into recesses of darkness.

His life is going to rot with hers,
his spine curved and cracking
under the weight of love.

Love at Eighty

These eyes have seen
the death of dreams, these hands
the curse of uselessness.

These two bodies curve from bones
grown porous, brittle
as dried leaves in autumn.

But love is fresh as crocuses in snow,
fragile as a dandelion,
wise to its mortality, the gift

of days too precious to waste
in anger or despair.
Old limbs twine

in love-knots to warm
the depths of winter, join a matched
tread of evening walks.

Old minds keep each other
company rummaging a treasure house
of memories, years now gone to fiction.

So little time, so much to discover
about what we were once,
what we might become.

Ghostwalk

The dust and bones of my people lie
among the rocks, the tangled grass
of neglected ground.

Headstones cede to valley rain, weathered
rock exposing runes in wrinkled
grooves of marble.

Mourner's paths have gone
to wilderness, their neat
borders a frayed fringe.

The tipsy gate that marked our plot
in Victorian curlicues has rusted
to a squeak,

graves folded to the bleak design of collapsing
coffin lids, bone husks
once named, now sewn to soil.

Perpetual care was promised,
the fate of hallowed bones trusted
to the security of Woodman Brotherhood.

It held no reprieve
from the lust of roots,
the restless heave of earth.

Reading Reminisce Magazine

I want to know it was all real,
that I did not imagine horse carts

lumbering down city streets,
that I was not the only child

who licked cream from milk bottle tops,
that others read by kerosene lamps,

our clean clothes smelled of Oxydol.
Tell me there is something left

if only in these wisps of memory.
Tell me those lost times, the loved faces

scored upon my brain are not fictitious.
I who live by disconnections

need to know that I am real.

In Retrospect

I'm thinking now of cousins
passed upon the street unrecognized,

aunts unseen since I was two,
a father who breathes in scribbled

longhand, a nephew whose freckles
are only photographic, my brother's

voice, a stranger's on the phone,
a niece who writes of her divorce

to names she assumes would care,
a mother whose distant life reads

like a Martian chronicle, and I am wondering
if blood is thinner than it used to be.

Small Deaths

I've said goodbye to furred
bodies laid with tender care
in fallow earth

to parent voices grooved
like ghostly melodies
upon the disc of childhood.

I've said goodbye
to summer lovers, their tanned
bodies, furtive smiles lost
in vanished moonlight,

to midnight vigils
pressed against the warmth
of infant flesh.

I've said goodbye
to places loved brick by blade
and folded time like antique
linen into chests of memory.

Azalea Ladies Club

I've watched their spines collapse
with the twist and curl
of drying leaves,

cracked discs skittering
in chaotic dance
down bony columns.

Through years their stomachs
pouf like marshmallows
swelling in hot ovens.

Sure strides turn to shuffle,
strolls to canes, high heels
to flat-soled platforms.

Their hands' smooth sheaths
grow pocked with hollows, tendons
strung with bulging knuckles,

their touch forever cool
as though blood somewhere
chilled into a clot.

Days accumulate in jowls
and wrinkles, years grow
long upon their faces.

From youth I've watched them, curious,
these cheerful friends of time
who do not fear decay.

Anatomy Lesson

This is the gizzard,
grandma said, poking a thick bulb
blooming in the viscera.

And this, she continued,
spinning out a skein of taffy-colored
tubes, t*his is the entrails.*

Now here, her finger indicated,
a great pearl set
deep in the ruby cavity,
we have the egg sack.

In the depths of grandma's porcelain
sink blood faded toward the drain
in sluggish opaque sheets.

On the plucked body dark roots
of each lost feather pimpled
the fragile skin.

Dimpled fat, grandma pried
from the flabby carcass floated like yellow
icebergs in the basin.

Perched on a kitchen stool
watching Sunday dinner move from barnyard
into oven, I felt smug knowing the secret way
a living thing is hinged.

Sharon **Scholl**, PhD professor emerita from Jacksonville University (Fl) where she taught humanities and non-western studies. Author of two scholarly books: *Music and Culture,* and *Death and the Humanities,* she has one book of poems, *Timescape,* in circulation. Recipient of Fulbright Fellowship and Witter-Bynner Foundation for Poetry Grant, she is an associate of the Atlantic Center for the Arts and active in local literary and music organizations.

www.ingramcontent.com/pod-product-compliance
Lightning Source LLC
Chambersburg PA
CBHW060227050426
42446CB00013B/3216